The diagram here explains the different nutrients and their role in the body. Only some of the vitamins and minerals your body needs are shown.

CARBOHYDRATES provide your body with the energy it needs physically (to move about) and internally (e.g. breathing, heart beating, brain working.)

WATER makes up a large proportion of the body; it transports substances and allows **chemical reactions** to take place in the body.

B VITAMINS help to release energy from food.

CALCIUM helps to make strong bones and teeth.

VITAMIN E helps keep the body healthy.

FATS protect your body from damage, provides **vitamins** A, D, E and K, helps keep us warm and supplies energy if it is not supplied by carbohydrate foods.

VITAMIN C helps to keep skin and gums healthy.

VITAMIN A helps eyesight and growth of the skin.

VITAMIN D works with calcium to build strong bones and teeth.

PROTEIN is needed to make new cells and repair any damaged ones. Protein is the main substance found in muscles, skin and internal **organs**.

IRON is important for giving blood cells their red colour.

5

What are carbohydrates?

There are three types of carbohydrate found in the diet: sugar, starch and **fibre**.

Sugars

Sugars are sometimes called 'simple carbohydrates' because they are made up of very small particles or **molecules**. A molecule is a very small part of a substance. Because they are so small, molecules of sugar are absorbed into our blood stream very easily when we eat foods that contain sugar. Sugars can be found in foods such as fruits, honey and even milk. These foods contain **natural sugars**. Sugars also come in a variety of forms, such as caster sugar, icing sugar and demerara sugar. These are added to other foods, for example, to biscuits. All types of sugar provide your body with energy.

Starches

Starches are more complicated than sugars so they take longer for your body to digest. During digestion all foods are broken down into molecules. When starches are broken down, they end up as molecules of **glucose**. Glucose is a sugar. So, starches are actually made up of lots of glucose molecules joined together. This means that starch also provides your body with energy. Foods containing starches include potatoes, rice, pasta, bread, couscous and polenta.

Carbohydrates can be found in a wide variety of foods.

CARBOHYDRATES

for a healthy body

Hazel King

www.heinemann.co.uk/library
Visit our website to find out more information about **Heinemann Library** books.

To order:
☎ Phone 44 (0) 1865 888066
▤ Send a fax to 44 (0) 1865 314091
▢ Visit the Heinemann Bookshop at www.heinemann.co.uk/library to browse our catalogue and order online.

First published in Great Britain by Heinemann Library, Halley Court, Jordan Hill, Oxford OX2 8EJ, part of Harcourt Education. Heinemann is a registered trademark of Harcourt Education Ltd.

© Harcourt Education Ltd 2003
First published in paperback in 2004
The moral right of the proprietor has been asserted.

Editorial: Jilly Attwood and Jennifer Tubbs
Design: Ron Kamen and Celia Floyd
Illustrations: Geoff Ward
Picture Research: Catherine Bevan, Rosie Garai and Liz Eddison
Production: Séverine Ribierre

Originated by Ambassador Litho Ltd
Printed in China by Wing King Tong

ISBN 0 431 16710 9 (hardback)
07 06 05 04 03
10 9 8 7 6 5 4 3 2

ISBN 0 431 16716 8 (paperback)
08 07 06 05 04
10 9 8 7 6 5 4 3 2 1

British Library Cataloguing in Publication Data
King, Hazel
Carbohydrates for a healthy body
613.2'83
A full catalogue record for this book is available from the British Library.

Acknowledgements
The Publishers would like to thank the following for permission to reproduce photographs: Action plus: p. **33**; Gareth Boden: pp. **8**, **11**, **12**, **17**, **21**, **23**, **30**, **31**, **34**, **35**, **37**, **42**; Getty/FPG: p. **40**; Gettyone Stone: p. **24**; Liz Eddison: pp. **6**, **7**, **9**, **13**, **20**, **28**, **29**, **38**, **43**; Robert Harrison: p. **4**; SPL/Quest: p. **16**; Trevor Clifford: p. **36**; Tudor Photography: p. **5**; Zefa: p. **39**.

Cover photograph of pasta reproduced with permission of Gareth Boden.

The author would like to thank Thomas King and Frank Reakes for their stories.

Every effort has been made to contact copyright holders of any material reproduced in this book. Any omissions will be rectified in subsequent printings if notice is given to the Publishers.

Contents

Any words appearing in the text in bold, **like this**, are explained in the glossary.

Why do we need to eat?

We all know which foods we enjoy. Eating can be great fun, especially midnight snacks or special treats, but have you ever stopped to wonder why we eat? Food is not there just for our pleasure; it is also needed to keep us alive and healthy.

Nutrients

All foods and drinks provide **energy** and **nutrients**. The main nutrients are carbohydrates, **fats** and **proteins**. Nutrients are needed to help your body grow and repair itself. This book is about carbohydrates, what they are and how the body uses them. You will need to find out about the other nutrients that your body needs to be healthy. Most foods provide a mixture of different kinds of nutrients but some provide more of one kind of nutrient than another. Your body needs nutrients every day; this is why you have to eat food. In addition, you must drink water, which, although not a nutrient, is essential for health.

Important roles

Each nutrient has an important job to do in the body. For example, you may know that carbohydrates provide the body with energy. Carbohydrates are provided by foods like bread, pasta, rice, sugar and potatoes. Fats also provide energy. Foods like butter, oil or margarine contain fats and a small amount of them can provide a lot of energy. Protein is provided by foods like meat, fish, eggs, nuts and lentils. It is needed to help make new cells throughout the body.

Eating a variety
Of course, not all foods contain all nutrients and some only contain them in small quantities. This is why it is important to eat a variety of foods every day.

Without the energy that food provides, leading a healthy active life would not be possible.

Choosing food

Today, most people can choose from a wide variety of foods. Lots of different foods are available, including ready-prepared and take-away meals.

Fibre

Fibre is the most complicated carbohydrate. Unlike sugar and starch, fibre does not provide you with energy but it does have an important role to play during the digestion of food. Foods that provide lots of fibre include any **wholemeal** or wholewheat products, such as bread, brown rice, pasta and some breakfast cereals. All fruits and vegetables, pulses (peas, beans and lentils), oats, barley and nuts will provide some fibre.

All the foods in this meal of pasta and vegetables, garlic bread, milk and fruit contain carbohydrates.

What is the carbohydrate in my food?

Food	Source of carbohydrate
pizza	pizza base
curry and rice	rice and any vegetables
spaghetti bolognese	spaghetti
beans on toast	beans and bread
lemonade/cola	sugar

Sugars and starches

Sugars

Many people say they have a 'sweet tooth' because they enjoy the taste of sweet foods. In Britain, foods have been sweetened for centuries. Honey was used by the Romans to add sweetness and to make drinks such as **mead**. Today there is a huge range of different sugars available to use in food preparation.

golden syrup

granulated sugar

caster sugar

maple syrup

icing sugar

sugar cubes

demerara sugar

honey

sugar crystals

muscavado sugar

Sugar comes in many different forms.

The role of sugars

Sugars can be very useful when preparing foods. For example, because sugars are sweet they are often added to savoury foods, such as tomato sauce, to make them more appealing. Sugars can be used to add colour to foods, either because brown sugar is used or because when sugars are cooked they turn a golden-brown colour. Sugars are used to **preserve** some foods, such as jam, and it makes food look attractive when used as an icing or decoration.

Starches

Starches are used in very different ways to sugars in the preparation of food. First of all, starches are not sweet. In fact, on its own a starch is quite bland; imagine eating raw flour! Most starchy foods have other ingredients added to them when meals are made. For example, pasta is served with a sauce, baked potatoes have a filling added and bread is made into sandwiches or toast.

Starches are still very useful when preparing food. Starches are able to thicken liquids. If potatoes are added to casseroles, the sauce will become less runny. Cornflour is another example of a starch being used to thicken foods. It can be used to thicken liquids or sauces and is also added to custard powder to help make custard.

Starches absorb (take in) liquids so, when rice or potatoes are cooked in a saucepan of water, they become soft because of the water they absorb. Starches can help to colour foods, for example, bread turns golden when it is toasted.

These starch-rich potatoes are being cooked in a saucepan by simmering them in water. The hard, raw potatoes absorb water during cooking and become soft.

Complicated fibre

Fibre is often referred to as the **complex carbohydrate** because it has a complicated structure. The human **digestive system** is unable to break it down so the body does not get any **nutrients** from fibre. But, the fibre is important because it helps the body's digestion. Fibre helps to make waste products soft and easy to pass out of your body. You will find out more about the digestive system on pages 14 and 15.

Insoluble fibre

There are two types of fibre: **insoluble fibre** and **soluble fibre**. The first is found in **bran** and products containing bran. Foods like **wholemeal** bread are made from wheat, which contains bran. It is known as insoluble fibre because it cannot **dissolve** in a liquid called ethanol.

Wholemeal or wholewheat products are sometimes called 'unrefined' foods. This means they have been left in a fairly natural state and have not been **processed**. Wheat, for example, can be processed so most of the outer bran is removed and the flour that is produced is white in colour. This type of flour provides some fibre. But if all the wheat grain is used (including the bran and **germ**) the flour that results contains a lot more fibre, which is helpful for your digestive system. Insoluble fibre passes through the body without changing very much at all. It can soak up liquids inside your body, and helps food move through your digestive system easily.

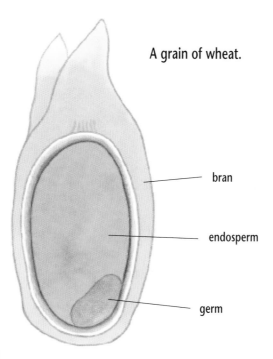

A grain of wheat.

bran

endosperm

germ

Fibre and cooking

When using ingredients that contain fibre you have to remember that they will act a bit differently. For example, if you make bread or pastry using wholemeal flour you must add extra liquid because the bran will soak up more liquid than white flour. Foods made with wholemeal or wholewheat flour will also tend to become dry more quickly than products made using white flour.

Oats are a good source of soluble fibre, so eating porridge for breakfast is a great start to the day!

Soluble fibre

The second type, soluble fibre, is found in foods like oats, vegetables and fruit. By including plenty of fruit and vegetables in your diet you keep your digestive system healthy. You will also benefit from the various **vitamins** and **minerals** that the fruit and vegetables provide.

Soluble fibre can help lower blood cholesterol levels. Soluble fibre in the diet can bind to bile acids which are released into the gut to aid the digestion of fat in the diet. The binding of bile acids to soluble fibre means that they are not able to be reabsorbed by the body to be used again. This means the body needs to make more bile acids, and this process uses up cholesterol, so helping to lower levels in the blood.

Energy efficient

You need energy

Carbohydrates are an excellent source of **energy**. Energy is needed so your body can grow, repair itself and keep warm. Even when you are asleep your body needs energy in order to function properly. Without energy you would not survive. You need it to breathe, **digest** food and even think! In fact, it is your brain that is the most energy-demanding **organ** in your body.

Every **cell** in your body needs the sugar called **glucose** and it is particularly important to your **nervous system**, red blood cells and brain. Glucose is the sugar that carbohydrates are broken down into when they are digested. After eating foods containing carbohydrates, some of the energy will be used straight away while the rest of it will be stored.

The human body uses 252kJ every hour just to sleep!

Glycogen stores

Any glucose that is not immediately needed by the body is stored in the **liver** or stays in the muscles. However, it is not stored as glucose. Instead it is converted into a substance known as **glycogen**. Carbohydrates are such a good source of energy because glycogen is quickly and easily turned back into glucose as soon as it is needed.

Measuring energy

The energy that is released from food is measured in **kilojoules** (**kJ**). Today this unit is usually used in schools and by **nutritionists** or **dieticians**, but food labels often still show energy values as **calories**. People can look at food labels to see how much energy will be provided by a meal or product.

Energy from food

All foods and most drinks provide energy. Water is one drink that does not supply any kilojoules. The amount of energy supplied by a food depends on what the food contains. Foods that are high in **fats** will have a high energy-value because fat provides the most kilojoules.

Food type	kJ per gram
carbohydrate	16
fat	37
protein	17

Carbohydrates and fats

It is interesting to compare the number of kilojoules that carbohydrate foods supply on their own and when combined with fats. For example, 100 grams of boiled potatoes provide 330 kilojoules. But when potatoes are made into chips (which means they are fried in oil) the energy values rise dramatically to 796 kilojoules.

All foods provide energy, but different foods supply energy in different amounts of kilojoules. Butter is higher in energy-value than meat or bagels.

Digesting carbohydrates

Carbohydrates may be a good source of **energy** but, until they have been broken down, your body cannot use the energy. The process of breaking down food is called digestion. After food has been **digested** it must be absorbed in a form that can be used by your body.

Chew it

The first stage of digestion takes place in your mouth. You physically start breaking down the food with your teeth by biting and chewing it. At the same time chemicals called **enzymes** in your saliva start attacking the starch. Enzymes are chemicals that speed up the breakdown of food. Large **molecules** in food are broken down into smaller ones. The saliva also makes the food moist and easier to swallow.

Swallow it

The moist, chewed up food is then swallowed and passes down a long tube called the **oesophagus** (see diagram). At the end of the oesophagus is the stomach, which is like a stretchy bag. Carbohydrate foods stay in the stomach for about two to three hours while being churned around and made into a mushy liquid called **chyme**. **Digestive juices** containing enzymes continue to attack the food and break it down.

Absorb it

The chyme gradually passes from the stomach into the **small intestine**, where further breakdown takes place. By now the food consists of tiny molecules, which are small enough to pass through the walls of the small intestine into the bloodstream (see diagram). You will find out more about absorption on pages 16 and 17.

Move it

You will see from the diagram that the digestive system is very long. Food cannot pass along it by itself – it needs some help. This help comes from the muscles in the walls of the intestines, which squeeze and relax, pushing the food along; a bit like squeezing some dough in your fist.

Release it

Any food that is not useful to the body will not be absorbed into the blood. Instead, it will pass from the small intestine into the **large intestine**. This is where any **insoluble fibre** will end up. As the remaining food particles travel along the large intestine, water is absorbed back into the body. Finally, waste matter is released from the body through the anus when you go to the toilet.

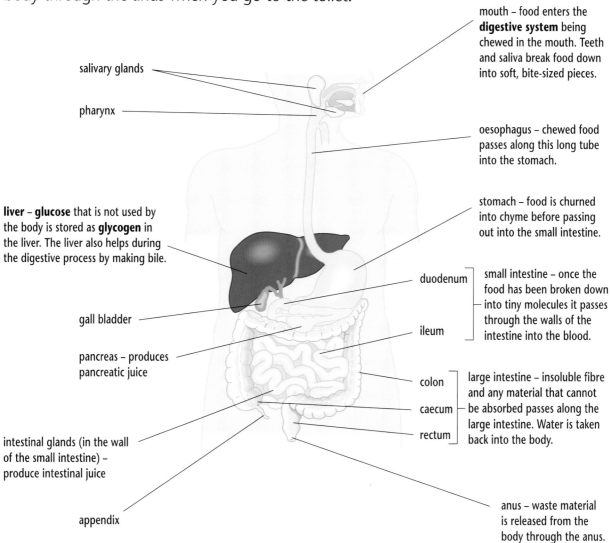

salivary glands

pharynx

liver – **glucose** that is not used by the body is stored as **glycogen** in the liver. The liver also helps during the digestive process by making bile.

gall bladder

pancreas – produces pancreatic juice

intestinal glands (in the wall of the small intestine) – produce intestinal juice

appendix

mouth – food enters the **digestive system** being chewed in the mouth. Teeth and saliva break food down into soft, bite-sized pieces.

oesophagus – chewed food passes along this long tube into the stomach.

stomach – food is churned into chyme before passing out into the small intestine.

duodenum

ileum

small intestine – once the food has been broken down into tiny molecules it passes through the walls of the intestine into the blood.

colon

caecum

rectum

large intestine – insoluble fibre and any material that cannot be absorbed passes along the large intestine. Water is taken back into the body.

anus – waste material is released from the body through the anus.

Food facts
Food can take at least 24 hours to travel through the intestines. When the intestines are stretched out, they are about as long as a double-decker bus!

Absorbing carbohydrates

The **nutrients** in the food that you eat need to get to all the **cells** in your body. There would be no point eating and **digesting** food unless your body had some way of getting the food into your bloodstream and transporting it around the body. The process that your body uses to do this is called absorption. This takes place in the **small intestine**.

Small intestine

By the time you are fully-grown your small intestine is about 7 metres long. It is made up of three parts: the **duodenum**, the **jejunum** and the **ileum**. Carbohydrates and **proteins** are absorbed in the jejunum, but **fats** are absorbed in the ileum. The small intestine looks like a folded tube that joins your stomach and your large intestine.

Tiny villi

The inside lining of the small intestine is covered with tiny hair-like projections called **villi**. There are millions of tiny villi on the inside of the small intestine. Each villus is about half a millimetre long and has even smaller 'microvilli' covering it! This is a very clever way to increase the surface area of the small intestine.

Surface area is the space occupied by the surface of something. This is easy to measure if something is flat, like a table, but to find out the surface area of the small intestine, the folded tube would have to be straightened out and each villi would have to be flattened. This is why the surface area of the small intestine is so much bigger than it first appears.

The lining of the small intestine is covered with villi, and the villi are covered with microvilli. Here you can see microvilli from the small intestine.

Molecules of digested food pass through the walls of the villi and into the blood vessels. It is important that all the food molecules are absorbed into your bloodstream so you can benefit from the nutrients. To do this, there must be as much surface area as possible to allow all the molecules to pass through the cell walls.

Molecules of food

When carbohydrate foods are broken down, the tiny **glucose** molecules are absorbed through the walls of the small intestine and into the blood. The blood transports the molecules to the liver for processing. The food molecules include glucose from the breakdown of carbohydrates, **amino acids** from the breakdown of **protein** and **fatty acids** from the breakdown of **fats**.

Leftover matter

Any food that remains after the absorption process has to be removed from the body. This sludgy matter contains the fibre that helps to keep the waste soft and bulky. This means it can leave the body more easily.

Your body gets water from the foods you eat and liquids you drink. Without water, the body would not be able to absorb nutrients from food.

Energy release

Food for fuel

Your body needs fuel to provide you with **energy** in the same way a car needs petrol or diesel to make it go. Carbohydrate foods are the best kind of 'fuel' for your body because they are broken down into **glucose**, which can be used by every **cell** in your body.

Your bloodstream is a bit like a car's petrol tank. It needs to have a constant level of glucose in the blood so cells can use it whenever energy is needed. It is the **liver's** job to decide whether there is the right amount of glucose in the blood. If there is more than your body needs, the liver changes the extra glucose into **glycogen** and stores it. The liver also changes the glycogen back into glucose as soon as the glucose energy in the blood is used up.

Turning food into fuel

The process of turning food into energy is a complicated process. Every cell in your body has a tiny 'energy factory' where a series of **chemical reactions** happen. The result is the release of energy. **Oxygen** is needed for this to happen properly. During this process **carbon dioxide** and water are produced. There is carbon dioxide in our breath when we breathe out.

The amount of energy you need depends on your weight, age, whether you are a boy or a girl and the type and amount of activity you are doing. Children and teenagers require a lot of energy compared to their size because their bodies are still growing. Boys tend to need more energy than girls and girls tend to have more body fat than boys. Different activities need different amounts of energy; running requires more than walking, but walking requires more than sitting. The weather can also affect your energy levels. If the weather is cold your body will have to work hard trying to keep you warm.

Turning food into fuel

People who are inactive are more prone to weight gain than those that lead active lifestyles. It is recommended that children and young people aim to do at least an hour of physical activity every day, and that adults aim to do at least 30 minutes of physical activity five days a week.

Constant levels

The best foods for keeping your **blood sugar levels** constant are those which contain **complex carbohydrates**. This is because they are gradually broken down and release their sugar slowly into the bloodstream. Wholegrain foods, beans, fruit and some vegetables are all slow-release carbohydrate foods. Sweets, on the other hand, cause blood sugar levels to rise quickly. This in turn makes the body try to lower the level. Blood sugar levels fall again creating a feeling of hunger. If more sweets are eaten the whole process starts again.

This diagram shows how energy is released from food when we eat.

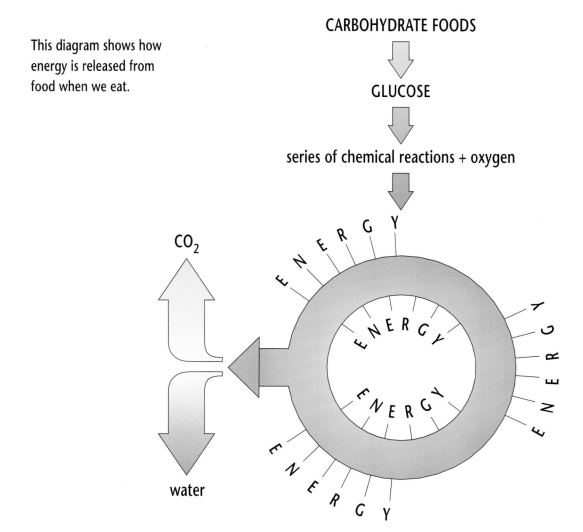

CARBOHYDRATE FOODS

GLUCOSE

series of chemical reactions + oxygen

ENERGY

CO_2

water

Energy and exercise

The amount of **energy** you need just to maintain your body, while you are doing absolutely nothing, is known as the **basal metabolic rate (BMR)**. The rate depends on the amount of muscle in the body. This means it will vary according to your weight, age and whether you are a boy or a girl. The BMR for a boy aged between ten and seventeen years and weighing about 70 kilograms is 7.84 **mJ** per day. For a girl of the same age and weight, her BMR will be about 6.69 mJ per day.

In and out

The energy your body receives from food is known as its energy input. The amount of energy it uses is its output. Ideally, the input and output should be roughly the same. However, if your energy input is higher than your output your body will store any extra as **fat** and you may put on weight. On the other hand, if your input is lower than your output you may lose weight. A good diet is one that ensures you stay at a healthy weight.

Energy you might need during various activities

Activity	Energy needed for one hour
running	2419 kJ
swimming	1612 kJ
walking	1083 kJ
sleeping	256 kJ

Today's advice on healthy eating recommends that most of your energy should be provided by carbohydrate foods.

Of course, you cannot work out how much energy you are going to use each day and then eat the right amount of food! Usually people rely on what their body is telling them and eat if they feel hungry and stop when they feel full. However, sometimes it is important to plan ahead, especially if you know you are going to do a lot of exercise. If, for example, you are going to do a lot of running you would know to fuel your body by eating meals containing pasta a few days beforehand.

Tom's story

Tom King uses plenty of energy doing various sports every week, including tennis, golf, cricket and swimming. However, his favourite sport is football. He plays forward for the California Boys in the East Berkshire League. He knows how to keep up his energy levels and stay healthy.

Tom says: 'I normally eat things like carrots, cucumber and lots of pasta. I have beans on toast before a big match and I only have crisps and fizzy drinks on special occasions (or when my mum lets me!)'

Body Fact

When running a **marathon**, your body starts off using blood sugar (**glucose**) then it uses **glycogen** stores. When glycogen runs out and, if no other energy is supplied, the body breaks down fat or **protein** to make its energy. However, this is much more effort for the body.

When you eat pasta, the energy that your body receives from it is released slowly.

Dental health

Today's healthy-eating advice tells us to reduce the amount of sugar we eat. If you often eat sugary foods your teeth can become damaged. Sugars left in the mouth attract **bacteria** that multiply resulting in the production of **acid**. Acid conditions cause tooth enamel to breakdown and teeth become damaged. This is known as dental caries ('caries' means 'rotten').

Brush well

After eating sugary foods your saliva helps the mouth to return to normal but this takes about thirty minutes. For this reason, if you do eat sweets, it is better to eat them all in one go rather than a few at a time. It is also better for your teeth if you choose sweets that can be eaten quickly. Sweets that are sucked give bacteria the conditions they enjoy for longer so they are likely to cause more damage. Of course, it is important to clean your teeth after eating any foods, especially sticky ones. Teeth should be brushed twice a day using a **fluoride** toothpaste.

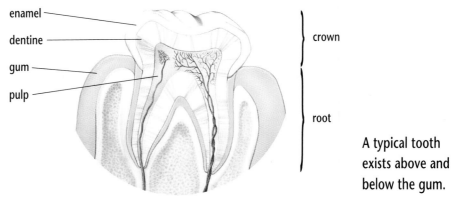

enamel
dentine
gum
pulp
crown
root

A typical tooth exists above and below the gum.

Inside, outside

Sugars can be divided into two categories; those found inside food **cells** and those that are not. The first type includes **glucose**, produced when carbohydrates are broken down, and fructose, which is found in some fruits. The second type includes the sugars used during baking (such as caster sugar, soft brown sugar and demerara sugar) as well as honey.

Health experts agree that a healthy diet should include only a small amount of foods containing fructose, the second type of sugar. This is because these sugars are found mainly in foods like cakes, biscuits, sweets, puddings, fizzy drinks and many ready-made meals. These foods tend to be high in sugars (as well as **fats**) and contain few **complex carbohydrates**.

Sweet treats

It is fine to eat sweets as a treat every now and then. However, although sugar provides your body with energy it does not provide any **nutrients**. Sugar does not contain **vitamins**, **minerals**, **protein**, starches, **fibre** or fats. This is another reason why health experts believe it is better to get energy from foods that also provide us with vitamins or other nutrients. When you are hungry it is better to choose fruit or a sandwich instead of sweets. You will gain more vitamins and minerals and it will be better for your teeth!

Always clean your teeth after eating foods containing sugar.

Too much of a good thing

Food is the fuel you need to give you **energy**, but food can also be fun! Other animals do not treat food in the same way that humans do. Animals tend to eat when they are hungry and only eat the food their body needs. People spend much more time thinking about food. They shop, prepare, cook and serve food. They can choose to eat at a restaurant or order meals from a take-away. Unlike animals, we have a great deal of choice when it comes to food.

Fast foods may be tasty but they are often high in fat.

Carbohydrate overload

Everyone is being encouraged to include plenty of **complex carbohydrate** foods in their diet. But the trouble with many of today's meals is that they also include lots of high-**fat** foods. A burger bun, for example, is a good source of starchy carbohydrate, but the burger inside is likely to be very fatty! A **wholemeal** bread sandwich sounds like a healthy option but if the bread is very thin and the filling includes lots of cheese and mayonnaise (both of which contain fat), then it is no longer such a healthy choice.

Healthy hearts

In 1999 the UK Government made targets for improving the nation's health. One of these targets was to reduce the amount of heart disease, or **coronary heart disease**. There are many reasons why people might develop heart disease and one of these is **obesity**. Obesity is when someone is very overweight. This not only affects their heart but can also affect the activities they are able to do.

The type of foods on offer today is part of the reason why there has been an increase in obesity and coronary heart disease. A lot of 'fast food' is high in fats and sugars and contains few complex carbohydrates. Food such as kebabs and burgers only fill you up for a short time so you feel hungry and need to eat again fairly soon.

Fat issue

Many people are overweight because of the high fat content of many of today's meals. Also people often snack rather than eat whole meals. This makes it easier to eat too much. Many snack foods are fried or contain a great deal of fat, such as chips, fried chicken and doughnuts.

Lack of exercise

As well as high fat meals, people do not exercise as much as they used to. Fewer young people walk to school because many households have a car and they spend more of their leisure time doing activities that do not require much energy, such as playing video and computer games. In addition to eating a healthy diet it is important to look after your body by taking regular exercise and getting plenty of fresh air.

Staying healthy

You will have read a lot so far about the importance of the **energy** supplied by starchy carbohydrate foods. However, they have many other health benefits too. **Complex carbohydrates**, such as those in wholegrain foods, beans, vegetables and fruit, can help reduce the risk of problems with the **digestive system**. This is because foods containing **fibre** help waste products travel through the digestive system (see pages 14 and 15). If there are no complex carbohydrates in the diet, the waste is not able to absorb moisture and becomes hard and dry. This makes it much more difficult for the waste to leave the body, leading to problems such as constipation.

Toilet trouble

Constipation is when someone has trouble going to the toilet. The waste matter (known as faeces or stools) is hard and does not travel easily through the digestive system. Sometimes this causes straining while on the toilet, which can then lead to **piles**. Another condition that can affect the digestive system is called 'diverticular disease'. This happens when pockets appear in the lining of the large intestine, or colon, into which waste material gets trapped. Eating complex carbohydrates may also help reduce the risk of getting bowel cancer later in life.

The large and small intestines

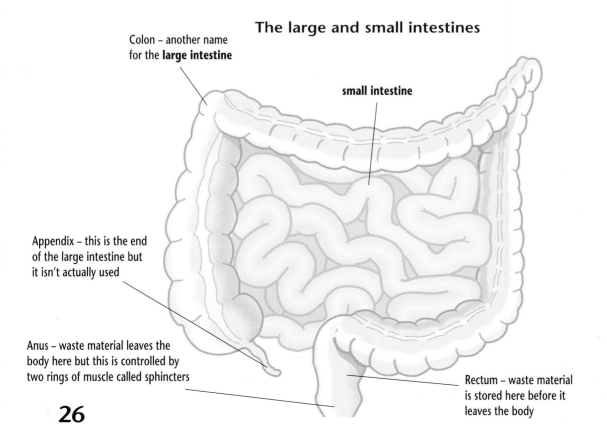

Colon – another name for the **large intestine**

small intestine

Appendix – this is the end of the large intestine but it isn't actually used

Anus – waste material leaves the body here but this is controlled by two rings of muscle called sphincters

Rectum – waste material is stored here before it leaves the body

Healthy carbohydrates

Following a diet that contains plenty of 'healthy' carbohydrates can also help reduce the chance of having appendicitis, which is what happens when the appendix becomes inflamed. Again, this is because waste material that is too dry becomes trapped in the appendix.

Not eating enough

Not eating enough food for a long time can be as harmful as eating too much. Your body needs a healthy balanced diet so that you can grow, repair yourself and do all the activities you want to do. People in **developing countries** do not always get enough food and may suffer diseases due to a lack of **nutrients**. Even in the western world where there should be enough food for everyone, people sometimes suffer because they are not eating the right things. If people do not have much money they may buy cheap foods that are filling, such as chips, and eat these every day. Chips provide energy in the form of carbohydrates and **fats**, but they do not provide much of the other nutrients. If somebody eats a diet low in nutrients for a long time they will become ill and their body will not grow properly.

Labelling sugar

Today people are being encouraged to try to reduce the amount of sugar they eat. This includes the sugar that is added to drinks or used in food preparation. The **natural sugars** found in fruits and some vegetables are not seen as a health problem.

All food products must be labelled to show their ingredients. This is useful for people who may want to eat certain foods or avoid certain foods, for example, sugar. But reading a food label is not always as easy as it sounds!

It contains what?

Many of today's ready-made meals and processed foods have to have extra ingredients added to them. It would not be possible to follow a cookery book recipe for apple pie and then expect it to stay fresh in the shops for a week. Products such as chocolate ice cream bars would not work unless extra ingredients were added. Sometimes **additives** are used to make foods last longer (preservatives) or to stop ingredients separating out (stabilizers).

Food fact

The ingredients listed below are from a chocolate ice cream bar containing caramel and nuts. They show that both sugar and glucose syrup are present in the caramel and in the ice cream.

Ingredients: Concentrated skimmed milk, milk chocolate (25%), caramel (8%) (concentrated skimmed milk, glucose syrup, sugar, vegetable fat, butteroil, stabiliser (E410), sugar, glucose syrup, vegetable fat, whey solids, wheat crispies, (1%) (wheat flour, salt, raising agent (E503), peanuts (1%) stabilizers, emulsifier, flavouring, colour.

You may be surprised by the foods that have sugar added.

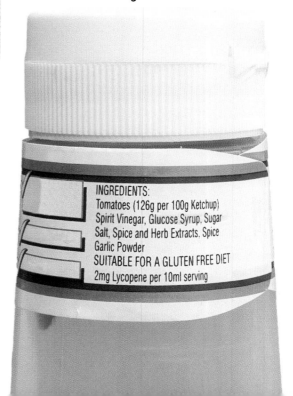

INGREDIENTS:
Tomatoes (126g per 100g Ketchup)
Spirit Vinegar, Glucose Syrup. Sugar
Salt, Spice and Herb Extracts. Spice
Garlic Powder
SUITABLE FOR A GLUTEN FREE DIET
2mg Lycopene per 10ml serving

Sugars are often added to food products, particularly those that have reduced **fat**. Sugar can help to make foods tasty and give foods 'body'. However, it is not always possible to tell how much sugar is in a product just by reading the ingredients list.

Sugars are often listed under their chemical names rather than just saying 'sugar'. For example, the following are all names of sugars: sucrose, glucose, lactose, fructose, invert sugar, syrup, molasses, honey and glucose syrup. This is why consumers do not always know exactly what they are eating or just how much sugar is contained in a product.

Sweet enough?

Many foods have added sweetness without the addition of sugar. Artificial sweeteners have been around for many years and they have the advantage of adding sweetness without adding **energy (kJ)**. Non-sugar sweeteners are particularly useful for people with **diabetes** who must be careful about the amount of sugar in their diet.

Many people use artificial sweeteners to avoid the **calories** in sugar or because they have to limit the sugar in their diet.

Food labels

The way food products are labelled, and the information put on the label, is carefully controlled by law. It is important that people are not misled by a food label, particularly someone who has an allergy to an ingredient. You will find out more about food allergies on page 34.

Food products must, by law, show the following information:

- a name
- a list of ingredients, starting with the heaviest and ending with the lightest
- a label to show shelf-life, such as 'best before' or 'use by'
- any special storage conditions or conditions of use
- the manufacturer
- where the food came from
- instructions for use
- weight or volume of the contents (unless it weighs less than 5 grams).

Packaged food must be accurately labelled so consumers know exactly what they are buying.

Food fact
Use by dates are used for foods that go off quickly and may be unsafe to eat after this date. These dates are found on foods like fresh meat, fish and cheese.

Best before dates are usually found on foods that will keep longer than a few days. They will not be at their best after this date. These dates are found on breakfast cereals, biscuits and tinned foods.

What's in a name?

All packaged food must have a name that tells people exactly what is in the package. For example, the label could not say just 'flour' because there are lots of different types of flour. It might say '**wholemeal** self-raising flour' or 'white plain flour' or even 'strong white bread flour'. The label must also say whether the food has been **processed**. So, a packet of pasta might have a label saying 'fresh' or 'dried' depending how it has been made.

Reading labels

You can also find different starches listed in ingredients lists. These are starches that have been used in food production. For example, starches such as cornflour can thicken sauces. Thickeners or thickening agents are often used in reduced-sugar or low-sugar products. Sugar usually makes things set (like jam for example). So, when less sugar is used something else is needed to act as a **gelling agent**. Maize starch (from sweetcorn) and potato starch are commonly used as thickeners and may be seen on many food labels.

Starch is needed to thicken food products, such as this white sauce being used to make lasagne. Different starches can be seen listed on food labels.

31

Sugar control

Glucose is your body's main source of energy. The way your body uses glucose is controlled by several chemicals called hormones. One of these hormones is insulin. Unfortunately for some people their bodies are not able to produce enough insulin. This means their bodies cannot control their blood sugar level. The amount of glucose travelling around in their blood can become very high or very low. The result is a disease called diabetes mellitus.

Diabetes mellitus

A very high or very low level of glucose in the blood is serious. The levels must be controlled. Diabetes mellitus can be controlled by either modifying the diet or by taking tablets and/or insulin. Some diabetics need a daily injection of insulin while others need only be careful about what they eat. A diet high in complex carbohydrates and fibre (including wholemeal bread, wholegrain rice and cereals, vegetables and fruit) is recommended because these foods help to control the rate at which sugar is absorbed into the blood.

Sweet treats

Someone with diabetes must make sure they do not have too much sugar or sugary foods and drinks, such as sweets, cakes, biscuits or fizzy drinks. Sugary products will cause a sudden rise in blood sugar levels. However, they do not have to avoid sweet foods altogether. They can eat sweet treats occasionally, but it is better to eat them after a meal rather than on an empty stomach. Products such as 'diabetic' chocolate are not usually necessary and often contain just as much fat and calories as 'ordinary' chocolate.

Young and old

It is not clear why people with diabetes do not make enough insulin in their bodies. There are two types of diabetes: young people's diabetes (or insulin dependent) and maturity onset diabetes (or non-insulin dependent.) The first type usually develops suddenly with severe symptoms and normally happens before the age of forty.

Non-insulin dependent diabetes does not require treatment with insulin because some insulin is still produced in the body. This type of diabetes can be controlled by eating healthily or sometimes by tablets. This type tends to affect middle-aged and older people, although anyone who is overweight is at a higher risk of developing the disease as they get older.

Frank's story

Frank Reakes is thirteen years old and was diagnosed with diabetes ten months ago. Frank says: 'Before I was diagnosed I noticed something was wrong; at school I couldn't concentrate and frequently asked to go to the toilet and get water. At home I was never hungry and I especially went to the toilet at night.' Having diabetes hasn't affected his lifestyle very much because he is still able to enjoy a variety of sports (football, hockey, badminton and skiing). The main changes he has had to make to his diet are avoiding snacks and puddings. He doesn't have sweet foods like ice cream and apple pie, except on Sundays. He also eats lots of complex carbohydrates like rice and pasta.

Having diabetes can affect the types of food you can eat, but you can still enjoy a wide variety of sports.

Food allergies

A food allergy is a reaction caused by eating a specific food or foods. Common foods most likely to cause an allergic reaction are milk, eggs, fish, shellfish, nuts and soya beans. Gluten is found in wheat, which is used to make flour, a carbohydrate food. Coeliac disease is the name for an intolerance to gluten.

Gluten

Gluten is a **protein** found mainly in wheat, although it is also present in rye, barley, oats and maize. People with coeliac disease have a condition in which the walls of their **small intestine** become damaged if they eat gluten. When the **villi** (see page 16) in the lining of the small intestine are damaged, **nutrients** are not absorbed properly. The symptoms include stomach pain, sickness, tiredness, bloating, diarrhoea and loss of weight.

Avoiding foods

Obviously someone with this allergy must avoid all foods containing gluten. Unfortunately this includes a huge range of foods because wheat is used to make flour. Just think how many products are made from flour: biscuits, cakes, most breads, pancakes, many sauces, pastries.

Anyone with coeliac disease must avoid foods like these, as they all contain gluten.

Lots of processed foods like desserts, snacks and ready-made meals contain starch-based thickeners containing gluten, so these must be avoided, too. Also, anything containing rye, barley or maize may cause a reaction, as well as foods made using oats, such as porridge and flapjacks.

Coeliac specials

Fortunately many supermarkets now cater for coeliacs and provide a range of gluten-free products. Many foods have gluten-free labels to show they are safe for coeliacs to eat. Health food shops have sold products, such as bread and cakes, for coeliacs for some time.

Food fact

Someone with coeliac disease will need to avoid some or all of the following: barley, bran, cereal filler, malt, modified starch, oats, rusk, rye, semolina, starch, wheat flour. This means they must read food labels very carefully.

Some foods are labelled 'gluten-free'.

Staple starches

A staple food is the main food of a diet and is usually a food that provides **energy**. Starchy carbohydrate foods are called staple foods because they form a major part of the diet. Different countries and cultures have their own staples depending on their climate and what they are able to grow. One of Britain's staple foods is wheat because the weather is suitable for growing it – wheat doesn't need lots of sunshine! So the diet of most British people was based on what could be made with wheat, or the flour made from wheat. Bread used to be an important filler (food that fills you up) that was fairly cheap for people to buy.

Today we have a huge variety of breads to choose from.

Potty about potatoes

Potatoes are also regarded as one of Britain's staple foods. Many traditional dishes are based on potatoes, such as Shepherd's Pie, Cottage Pie, sausages and mash and potato cakes. Even today many people would not consider a meal complete unless it was served with potatoes.

Lots of choice

Today you do not have to rely only on foods that can be grown and produced in this country. There are now many ways to **preserve** food so that it will keep longer including while it is transported from another country. This means you have a much wider choice of foods on offer. If you want bread you can now choose between ciabatta (from Italy), croissant (from France), rye bread (from Germany) or naan bread (from India). It is also now possible to make these products in England, so you may see croissants labelled 'made in England'.

Pass the pasta

Pasta is traditionally a staple food of Italy. It can now be bought fresh or dry or as part of a ready-made meal. Pasta is made with flour and sometimes eggs are added. The flour used for pasta making comes from durum wheat. This produces semolina flour, which is fine, gritty and yellow in colour. Once the pasta dough has been made it is cut, pressed and moulded into different shapes and sizes.

Pasta parties

Pasta is a very healthy food. It is low in **fats** and high in **complex carbohydrates**. It even has a 'high **fibre**' version – brown pasta provides more fibre. Many athletes eat plenty of pasta before a big event – they may even have a pasta party the evening before!

Pasta comes in a huge range of shapes, sizes and colours!

Worldwide diets

Rice is a staple food of several countries including India, China and Japan. Like pasta, rice is low in **fat** and high in **complex carbohydrates**. Brown rice contains **bran** so it also provides **fibre** and has slightly more **protein**, iron, calcium and B **vitamins**.

Rice dishes

There are many different varieties of rice. So it is not surprising that there are also many different ways of cooking and serving rice. Traditionally in Britain, short grain pudding rice was soaked in milk and cooked slowly in the oven to make a rice pudding. In India long grain rice is cooked in stock (flavoured liquid) with meat, fish and/or vegetables to make a pilau. Japanese and Chinese dishes tend to use soft, sticky rice that can be shaped with the fingers (as in sushi) or picked up with chopsticks. The Italians are famous for risotto. Ladles of stock are slowly added to the risotto rice until it becomes creamy, plump and tender.

Cornmeal made from maize can be used to make polenta and cornbread.

Gluten free

Rice is also similar to pasta because it is a 'slow-release' carbohydrate so it is a much better source of **energy** than the 'instant' energy provided by sugary foods. In addition, rice is suitable for people with coeliac disease because it does not contain any gluten.

Puffed rice

Rice is not only eaten as grain in savoury and sweet dishes, but it can also be **processed** to make many other products. Grains of rice can be ground up to turn them into rice flour, ground rice and flaked rice. These ingredients are then used to make puddings, cakes, biscuits and as thickening agents for soups or stews. Rice can also be 'puffed' to make puffed rice cereals and rice cake snacks.

Moroccan couscous

Couscous is the name of a tiny grain made from finely ground semolina wheat. It cooks very quickly in hot water or by being steamed. Today you can buy packets of dried couscous, some of which have flavours already added to them. Couscous is also the name of a spicy Moroccan dish which is served on a bed of couscous. Traditionally couscous was a staple food of North Africa.

Maize or corn?

Maize (also called corn) is a staple food of many countries including Italy, Mexico and the USA. It can be used to make a wide range of products, such as tortillas (thin pancakes), polenta (a dough made from maize flour), cornbread, breakfast cereals and even popcorn!

Couscous can be used as an alternative to rice.

Eating for health

Most people would like to be healthy and free from disease all the time. This is important, not just for individuals but for the country as a whole. It is better for people, and cheaper for governments, to prevent diseases happening rather than treating them once people are ill.

Food fact

In the UK, the Food Standards Agency say the key to a healthy diet is to eat a variety of foods. For most people this means eating:

- **more fruit and vegetables – eat lots! You can choose from fresh, frozen, tinned, dried or juiced**
- **more bread, cereals and potatoes – these should make up about a third of your diet**
- **less fat and sugar – try to eat and drink less of these sorts of foods.**

Preventing disease

It is now known that the diet you eat throughout your life can affect your risk of getting diseases such as **coronary heart disease**. **Dietary guidelines** have been produced to help people choose a diet that contains foods needed for good health. These guidelines do not tell people *what* to eat but suggest different ways to follow a healthy diet. Dietary guidelines are produced by various health organizations, including governments.

Varied diet

Eating a variety of different foods is particularly important. People sometimes end up eating the same foods every day out of habit, laziness or just because they like them. But in the long term this can lead to a lack of some **nutrients** and could cause health problems. There is not one single food that contains all the nutrients in the right quantities, which is why everyone should eat a variety of foods. When you think about the thousands of foods available it must be possible to find different ones that you like to eat.

Drinking plenty of water is also part of a healthy diet.

Balance of health

To help people understand about eating healthily in the UK, the Balance of Good Health was produced. It is used by dieticians, health professionals, manufacturers, caterers and in schools. However, it is not recommended for very young children or some people under medical supervision. The Balance of Good Health clearly shows the sort of foods that can be included in a healthy diet and in what proportion. For example, the section containing foods providing carbohydrate is quite big, while the section showing fatty and sugary foods is much smaller.

The 'Balance of Good Health' plate shows the proportions of different foods that make up a healthy diet.

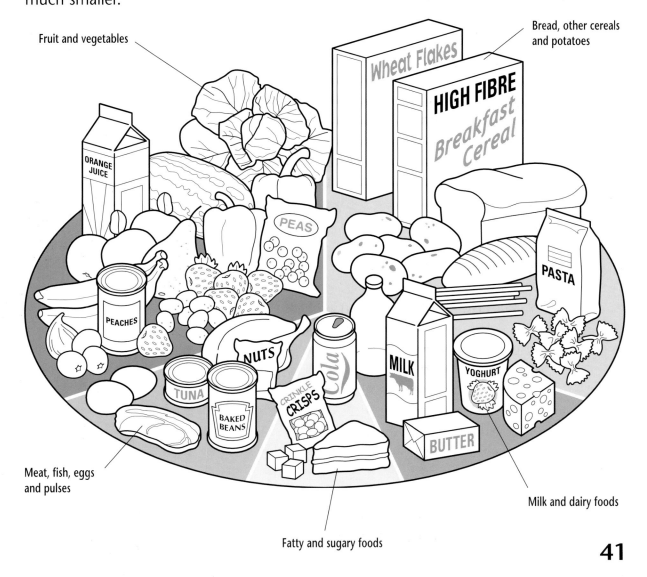

Fruit and vegetables

Bread, other cereals and potatoes

Meat, fish, eggs and pulses

Fatty and sugary foods

Milk and dairy foods

Achieving a balance

Eating a healthy diet is not just about the foods you choose. It is also about the way those foods are prepared and cooked. Potatoes are high in **complex carbohydrate** and provide **vitamin** C. But if potatoes are cut into thin slices and deep-fried, they will also contain lots of **fat**. Or, if the potatoes are boiled then left to go cold and reheated, any vitamin C present is likely to be lost. This is because vitamin C **dissolves** into the cooking water and is destroyed by heat. So, it is important to consider how foods are cooked.

Thick chips

Eating a healthy balanced diet does not mean you have to give up foods you enjoy. It just means you shouldn't eat them all the time. Eating chips occasionally is fine and it is even better if you can choose thick chips! If a potato is cut into 'thick chips' rather than thin ones, it will absorb less fat when cooked.

Lots of foods can be just as tasty if they are cooked without using or adding fat. Eggs are a good example. They can be boiled, poached or scrambled. Bacon is best grilled because the fat can drip into the grill pan so you do not have to eat it. Some foods can be 'dry fried' which means no extra fat is added to the pan. There are some good non-stick frying pans which make this method possible.

Potatoes can be eaten in a variety of ways; as long as you don't always eat fatty chips you can enjoy a healthy variety.

Saving vitamins

Vegetables are often cooked by boiling them in water. Some vitamins dissolve into the water during cooking and are lost when the vegetables are drained. It is better to steam or microwave vegetables as less water is needed and more of the vitamins are saved.

A healthy balanced diet should be part of everyone's lifestyle.

Carbohydrate in a variety of foods broken down into starch, sugars and fibre.

Food	Starches (grams)	Sugars (grams)	Fibre (grams)
1 banana	15.3	1.5	2.0
1 small can baked beans	9.7	2.8	6.9
100 grams cauliflower	0.2	1.8	1.6
2 slices bread, brown	41.3	3.0	5.9
2 slices bread, white	43.8	3.0	3.7
1 slice sponge cake	22.0	30.4	1.0
100 grams flour, wheat, white, plain	76.2	1.5	3.6
100 grams flour, chapatti, white	75.6	2.1	4.1
100 grams golden syrup	0.0	79.0	0.0

Information adapted from *Food Tables & Labelling*, New Edition (see Resources list).

Glossary

acid   something that tastes sour, for example vinegar or lemon juice

additives   substances (natural or artificial) added to foods to increase their shelf-life or to improve their colour, flavour or texture

amino acids   building blocks of proteins. Different amino acids combine together to form a protein.

bacteria   micro-organisms (living things) that are so small they can only be seen through a microscope. Some are helpful, like those in our intestines and some can be harmful, such as those that cause food poisoning.

basal metabolic rate (BMR) rate at which your body burns food when it is completely rested

blood sugar level   amount of glucose in the blood. This will rise after sugar has been eaten and will gradually fall until food is eaten again.

bran   the outer layer of a grain of wheat

calories   measurement of energy supplied by food

carbon dioxide   gas present in our breath when we breathe out

cells   microscopic living things that make up all living matter

chemical reaction   something that occurs between two or more chemicals

chyme   mushy liquid which passes from the stomach to the small intestine. It is formed from partly digested food mixed with the digestive juices of the stomach.

complex carbohydrates carbohydrates that cannot be broken down by the human digestive system, such as the bran in wholemeal bread

coronary heart disease   illness that effects the heart – when the vessels leading to the heart become blocked by fatty substances the blood cannot get to the heart as easily

developing countries   poorer countries that do not have well established industries and services, such as transport, schools, welfare

diabetes   when the body does not have enough insulin (a hormone) to control the amount of glucose in the blood

dietary guidelines   suggestions for healthy eating

dietician   person who advises people about what they eat

digest   process of breaking down food when it is eaten. Digestion starts in the mouth when you bite and chew food and continues until the molecules that make up food are taken into the bloodstream.

digestive juices   liquids containing enzymes that help to break down food during digestion – saliva and gastric juice are examples of digestive juices

digestive system   all the parts of the body which are used to digest food

dissolve   to gradually disappear in a liquid

duodenum   first part of the small intestine

energy   what the body needs to stay alive. Energy is supplied by foods.

enzyme   something that helps a chemical reaction to take place faster without being changed itself

fats   nutrients in a wide range of foods, especially fatty ones

fatty acids   small units that fat is broken down into during digestion

fertilizer   chemical or natural substance added to soil to provide nutrients for plant growth

fibre   name for the parts of a carbohydrate that your body cannot break down – it is found in wholewheat foods, bran, the skin of fruits and vegetables and baked beans

fluoride   mineral often added to toothpaste to help build strong teeth

gelling agent   something that helps a food product set, and gives it shape and structure

germ   part of the wheat grain. It contains some of the vitamins and fats.

glucose   smallest unit that carbohydrates can be broken down into during digestion

glycogen   name for any glucose stored in the liver and muscles following absorption – extra glucose is stored if it is not needed immediately by the body

hormones   substances produced by different glands in the body that affect or control particular organs, cells or tissues

ileum   third and last part of the small intestine

insoluble fibre   type of fibre which will not dissolve

jejunium   middle part of the small intestine

kilojoules (kJ)   measurement of energy supplied by food

large intestine   the part of the intestines through which undigested food passes after it has left the small intestine

liver   organ in the body used in the digestive system

marathon   long distance running race

mead   fermented drink made out of honey

minerals   nutrients needed by the body in small amounts

megajoules (MJ)   a very large measurement of kilojoules (MJ = 1 million joules)

molecules   very small parts of a substance

natural sugars   sugars naturally present in food, not added

nervous system   series of connected nerves throughout the body

nutrients   carbohydrates, proteins, fats, vitamins and minerals are all nutrients. Foods and most drinks contain different amounts and types of nutrients.

nutritionist   person who studies nutrients and how the body uses them

obesity   state of being extemely overweight

oesophagus   the tube through which food travels from the mouth to the stomach

organ   internal body part, such as the liver, stomach or an intestines

oxygen   gas present in the air and used by the body when we breathe in

piles   collection of swollen veins around the anus caused by a diet low in fibre which leads to straining

preserve   to protect food from going 'off' food can be preserved for a short time by cooking it or putting it in the fridge, or it can be preserved for longer by freezing, canning, bottling, vacuum packing, jamming, irradiating, drying, pickling or adding preservatives

processed   describes foods that have been changed to make them easier to prepare, cook and/or eat

proteins   nutrients supplied by foods such as meat, fish, and nuts

small intestine   part of the intestine into which food passes from the stomach to be digested and absorbed into the blood. Undigested food passes right through the small intestine into the large intestine.

soluble fibre   fibre that can be dissolved

villi   tiny bumps in the intestines through which digested food and water is absorbed

vitamins   nutrients needed by the body in small amounts

wholemeal   food that uses the whole of the wheat grain

Resources

Books

Digestion: How we fuel the body, Angela Royston (Franklin Watts, 1998)

Food Tables and Labelling, A. E. Bender and D. A. Bender
(Oxford University Press, 1999)

Websites

www.coeliac.co.uk/
Provides information about coeliac disease.

www.diabetes.org.uk
Provides information and leaflets about diabetes.

www.eduack.com
The Eating Disorders Association provides information and leaflets.

www.fabflour.co.uk
Provides information and resources about wheat and flour.

www.potato.org.uk
Provides information about potatoes as well as recipes.

www.food.gov.uk
The UK government's website for the Food Standards Agency. The 'Your daily diet' section gives advice about healthy eating.

Contacts

Diabetes UK
10 Queen Anne Street
London
W1G 9LH
020 7323 1531

The Coeliac Society
PO Box 220
High Wycombe
Bucks   HP11 2HY
01494 437278

Eating Disorders Association
First Floor, Wensum House
103 Prince of Wales Road
Norwich
Norfolk   NR1 1DW
Youth Helpline 01603 765050

The Flour Advisory Bureau Ltd
21 Arlington Street
London
SW1A 1RN
020 7493 2521

Disclaimer

All the Internet addresses (URLs) given in this book were valid at the time of going to press. However, due to the dynamic nature of the Internet, some addresses may have changed, or sites may have ceased to exist since publication. While the author and Publisher regret any inconvenience this may cause readers, no responsibility for any such changes can be accepted by either the author or the Publisher.

Index